The Journey From Oz

Seven Steps For Finding Your Way Back From Places You Never Intended To Be

Sharon Murphy Yates
Illustrated by Rose-Ann San Martino

The Journey from Oz

A product of Encouragement Ink

ISBN-13: 978-0615579269

ISBN-10: 0615579264

THE JOURNEY FROM OZ

SEVEN STEPS FOR FINDING YOUR WAY BACK
FROM PLACES YOU NEVER INTENDED TO BE.

Sometimes in life,
the skies turn gray
and cold winds blow
tough times our way...
swept up in events,
tossed about helplessly,
we find ourselves
in places
we never
intended
to be.

INTRODUCTION

It happened to Dorothy when she landed in Oz, and it can happen to anyone. There are times in all our lives when unexpected events come along, spin us around and slam us down in places we never thought we would be. It may be the direct result of things you have done, or as random as lightning on a cloudless day. For Dorothy, that place was Oz. For you, it could be any aspect of your life - emotional, physical, financial, mental or spiritual.

It doesn't matter how you got here. What matters now is finding your way to the place you would rather be. This book offers a way to do that. There is help and hope available. No matter what circumstances surround you or how hopeless the situation may seem, there **are** things you can do.

When confronting challenges we have two options: we can passively accept whatever happens, or we can actively acknowledge the challenge as an opportunity for learning to appreciate life more fully. There's always a choice. What you do with that choice is up to you, but remember this: if you **want** something different, you may need to **do** something different.

As difficult as the road ahead may seem…as difficult as it may really be…every step forward is worth taking. You owe it to yourself and to all the people who care about you (and there are always more than you realize) to make this journey. One step at a time…one day at a time…you can do this. So breathe in, breathe out, put one foot in front of the other, and let's get started!

Step One:

Assess the Situation

(Where Has Your House Landed?)

The first step in addressing any challenge is to assess the situation. When Dorothy's house crashed in Oz, she didn't hide under the bed. She picked herself up, stepped outside, and looked around to see where she was. If you want to find your way to a better place, you need to do the same thing. You have no hope of finding your way to a better place until you are willing to open your eyes and take an honest look at where you are.

* * *

Some say ignorance is bliss. It's not true. It never was. It never will be. The more information you have, the better equipped you are to deal with any situation. You are where you are. Make the decision to take responsibility for that, and you immediately begin to take the first steps toward regaining control of your life. It's a huge step in the right direction.

* * *

Things can and do get better. It may not happen overnight, but the sooner you start to collect the facts and assess your situation, the sooner you can begin to move beyond it. Even if you feel you've reached the depths of despair, you have to understand this is just a dark place you're passing through. No one has to take up permanent residence here.

* * *

We all face challenges in life. We expect that. For the most part, we've probably done pretty well in facing them and overcoming them. However, sometimes life can take twists and turns we didn't anticipate. Dorothy is a good example. One minute she's skipping along life's path, dealing with nothing more than minor aggravations and the next, everything is spinning out of control. That may be how you feel right now. Sometimes our worlds spin for a while before we can regain our balance. Hold on tight. You'll get through this.

* * *

Even if you feel battered from the storms that brought you here, this isn't the time to give up or give in to feelings of helplessness. You may need some time to rest and adjust and recover, but the sooner you start to do SOMETHING, the sooner you can begin to take back some control over the direction of your life.

As you gather information, new options may begin to appear. If you want to be somewhere other than where you are in life right now, you have to start making the choices that are going to take you there. Good information makes it easier to make good choices. You can take off in a random direction hoping you'll get there, or you can spend some time gathering the information you need to find the best route. Having the information you need reveals the most direct path to where you want to be.

* * *

You'll be more successful in finding your way to a better place if you recognize the traps that prevent you from moving forward. When a crisis hits home, you can spend a lot of time wondering why life is so unfair. If you aren't careful, you'll get stuck in a victim's role. Life can be **very** unfair…but fairness is rarely a factor in changing circumstances. Your inability to move beyond the "fairness factor" will only postpone any positive action. Fair or unfair, the situation is what it is. When you accept that, you are ready to start doing something about it.

* * *

It's easy to get caught up in the process of looking outside of ourselves for answers. Like Dorothy, we look for wise and wonderful wizards to solve our problems. We look for wicked witches to blame for our problems. When we look to others to be responsible for our lives, we give them the power. It keeps us from taking the time to look at what **we** could be doing to make things better. When we accept responsibility for our lives, we give ourselves the power to change them. You cannot gain control of your life if you are constantly giving your power away. Read that again because it's important. You cannot gain control of your life if you are constantly giving your power away.

* * *

Sometimes our view of what our life should be is a lot like Dorothy's ideas about that perfect "over the rainbow" place. You only complicate your life when you depend on other people to define the perfect life for you. Let go of unrealistic expectations. You can be so determined for things to be the way you want them to be that you completely ignore any evidence to the contrary. If you want to move forward, you need to look at the facts. Honestly acknowledging the truth of our lives isn't easy, but it's one of the most beneficial things we can do.

* * *

When you face difficult times, one of the most important things you can realize is that we define our lives by the choices we make. Every choice matters. Choosing well often depends on your ability to recognize **all** the choices that are available to you.

* * *

The answers we need to find our way are usually within reach. The thing that gets in our way is being open enough to recognize them and expectant enough to receive them. Part of the problem is that we don't always want the answers that come. We think we know the **best** solution, and we set our minds on that being the **only** solution. Open your mind to the potential of new possibilities. There may be options for better outcomes than you ever imagined. If you want to find your way to a better place, it's time to start paying attention to the results **you** want and the choices **you** make. Life is a trial and error evolutionary process. It is what it is until you make it something better.

* * *

Stop thinking in terms of failure when things don't go the way you planned. Think of the things that go wrong as life lessons. As children, we know we often have to try things many times before we master them. We are taught that the most important lessons generally take the most time and effort and learning the most difficult lessons is usually the most rewarding. As adults, we tend to forget this. When things don't work out the way we want them to we may forget the importance of learning from it. The greatest stories of inspiration you'll ever hear will have one factor in common; the hero of those stories did not let adversity stop them; they used it to become stronger. If you can shift your focus from your limitations to your potential, your chances for success soar!

* * *

You are not the tornado. You are not the disease or disaster or failure or disappointment or any other unwanted event that may have come into your life. The storms that have passed through or remain in your life may help define who you become, but they are not who you are. Don't see yourself as anything less than everything you are.

A few words on packing for your journey…

Let's talk about packing for your journey to a better place. The women in my family are famous for over packing. Even in my backpacking days, I had the tendency to take things I didn't need. When you are backpacking - a lot like in life - you are literally carrying all that extra stuff around on your back, and it can weigh you down and slow your progress.

My husband has a simple solution for it. He says, "Figure out what you need and leave the other crap behind." That's good advice for dealing with challenges too.

Take some time to think about the attitudes, fears and beliefs that have kept you from moving forward in the past. Nothing can hold you back more than your own mindset about moving forward. Once you become aware of your personal anchors to the places you don't want to be, you can start to take actions to free yourself from them.

Leave the lying behind. Stop pretending you believe things you know aren't true. It could be lies someone else is telling you or lies you are telling yourself. Lies keep us from moving forward. You can't start this journey until you're willing to be honest about it.

Look at the ways you've handled challenges in the past. If the tools you've been using to try and fix things in the past haven't worked, stop thinking they will work the next time. Albert Einstein said, "The definition of insanity is doing the same thing over and over again and expecting a different result." We get caught in patterns of responses that may have disastrous consequences for us each time we resort to them, yet we continue to use them. If you want to get out of a rut, you might want to put down the shovel you've been using and think about finding a ladder instead. Or, if every time you react with anger it brings you negative results, maybe you need to try something different. Recognize the things that don't work and leave them behind.

Finally, leave the "I've got to please everybody" attitude behind. It's not even possible. This is about you. You cannot change anyone but yourself. You cannot judge what is perfect for you by what appears to be perfect for others. You cannot take care of other people until you take care of yourself. Find out what you need and leave the other crap behind.

Okay. All unpacked and ready to go? If so, you are ready for the next step. You're ready to start doing what you need to do. You CAN do this!

Step Two:

Take Steps in the Right Direction

(Finding Your Own Yellow Brick Road)

* * *

To change anything about your life, you need a plan. Not that "running in circles and screaming like your hair is on fire" kind of plan (and yes, you've seen it and know exactly what I'm talking about). You need a real plan of action. Even in situations where you feel you have little, if any, control, you can achieve greater success in surviving it with a plan.

* * *

When Dorothy landed in Oz, she had to decide where she wanted to go from there. As you get a better idea about where you want to be (and keep in mind, this is an ongoing process), set some goals for yourself.

* * *

Goals guide your path on your personal yellow brick road. Your goals may be small at first, depending on what you are able to do. It doesn't matter if your beginning goals are as simple as getting out of bed and getting dressed, scheduling an appointment or making a phone call. It's important to start doing **something**.

* * *

The biggest reason most people feel lost in life is they haven't taken the time to plan where they want to go. You can have detailed maps, OnStar navigation or a Sherpa guide sitting by your side, but if you don't know where you want to go, it's not going to help. Most of us put more thought and attention into planning a vacation than we do in planning our lives.

* * *

If you don't take time to put some serious, passionate, specific thought into deciding where you want to be, you're not likely to recognize it when you get there. The sooner you know, the less time you will spend going down the wrong roads to find it.

* * *

You can choose to move forward as soon as you are ready to stop making excuses for not doing it. Stop limiting yourself with self-imposed boundaries.

* * *

Every challenge provides an opportunity to examine our lives, and appreciate who we are. Even events where we feel completely helpless can be opportunities to decide to do some things differently.

* * *

When you set goals, you need to establish some priorities. Think about what you need to do first. What are the immediate needs? Obviously, if your Scarecrow is on fire, you need to deal with that before moving on to less urgent tasks.

* * *

Make a list of things you need to do. A written list focuses your time, attention and energy in one direction. It also gives you a sense of accomplishment as you complete each task and check it off.

* * *

When you evaluate the options for finding your way to a better place, keep an open mind. Crisis and challenges are opportunities to learn and grow. The situations happening in your life right now may not be the path you would have chosen if given the chance, but there is something for you to gain from it if you can be open to that possibility.

* * *

Taking the first steps to a better place can be tough. The possibility of taking your life to new places can be almost as scary as staying where you are. No matter how uncomfortable, unproductive or painful life gets, we tend to cling to the things we know rather than seeking something new. For most of us, things have to be really bad before we are ready to make changes. We can tolerate a lot, so we forget that we don't have to.

* * *

Traveling through new places can be lonely. When her house first crashed in Oz, every munchkin in the land came out to show support, offer advice and cheer Dorothy on (even if some just showed up out of curiosity). Once she started trying to find her way, she was out there on her own. It can be hard, painful and lonely at times, but don't let that stop you. This is worth doing.

* * *

When Dorothy started out on the yellow brick road it just went around in circles at first. You may feel like that right now. In the beginning, it can take real effort to make any progress.

* * *

Some situations are so overwhelming it may seem like ten minutes at a time is all you can handle. So handle those ten minutes…and then the next ten minutes…and the next. Do what you can do until you can do better. It will get easier.

* * *

Do not resent or resist the fact that there are people who may know more than you do about some things. Take advantage of it.

* * *

Everyone needs a little help sometime. Sometimes we need a lot of help! Don't be afraid to ask for the help you need.

* * *

Knowledge is power. Use that power to start taking action. The action you take will reduce your feelings of helplessness and hopelessness and start to restore a sense of confidence in your ability to take control of your life and overcome whatever challenges you face.

* * *

Find out about the resources, people, programs and agencies that are available to assist you. They're out there; it's just a matter of finding them.

* * *

Talk with people who have encountered similar situations. We can benefit from the experience, strength and hope of others.

I'm out of bed and have clean underwear on!

* * *

When my best friend was going through a very difficult personal crisis, we celebrated the fact that she could motivate herself enough to get out of bed and get dressed. I would call and say, "How's today?" and she would say, "Well, I'm out of bed, and I've got clean underwear on." At the time, that was a big deal. It meant she hadn't given up. She was doing what she could do at that point in time. That's what you do when you start to take steps to bring yourself to a better place. You do what you can do. It may not be much in the beginning, but you do what you can do until you can do more - whatever that is for you.

* * *

There may be some things you can't do **anything** about right now. Don't dilute your efforts by wasting time and energy on things you cannot change. This isn't the time to get lost in the land of could have, should have, would have.

* * *

You can't move forward if you're constantly looking back. If there is something you can do to right the wrongs of the past, do it. If there's not, learn from it and move on.

* * *

When you begin the process of following your own yellow brick road, you may not even see the road at first. That's okay. Do what you can. Breathe in, breathe out, get out of bed and put on clean underwear. Big changes start with small steps.

* * *

Sometimes, there will be setbacks. Changing any behavior or situation is a process. No matter how well you are doing, it is always possible to relapse. Don't let a setback defeat you. Remember this: life is full of second chances (and even third and fourth chances). There are more options and opportunities in life than you ever realized. Even if you've traveled down some wrong paths in the past, wrong doesn't have to mean wasted. The lessons we learn from the journey – if we choose to learn from them – can help to uncover the true gifts in our lives. This is just a place you're passing through. You're on your way to better things. Keep going!

Step Three:

Finding the Help You Need

(We're Off to See the Wizard)

* * *

It's okay to admit we need help. No one helped Dorothy until she admitted she was lost and needed help to find her way. The Scarecrow, Lion and Tin Man all began their journeys by admitting there were things they wanted to be different. You could spend years stuck in a field, rusting by the side of the road, or afraid of everything around you, OR you can decide to do the things you need to do to make the differences you want to make. It is never too late to make the decision to change. Never.

* * *

Knowing what you need to do and knowing how to do it are two different things. You may have been successful in handling everything in your life on your own up to this point, but there are things in life that inevitably stop us in our tracks. Don't worry. Sometimes it results in detours that may lead us in a better direction.

* * *

Unless someone has just given you a magic wand, this is probably going to take some time. Coping with challenge and change is a profoundly personal experience with a timetable all its own. Your pace may not be the same as someone else's. Some days will be better than others. Be patient with yourself. It will get easier.

* * *

People who want to help you may not know what to do. Help them to know what you need, and you will help yourself. I believe it's important to say things out loud. Start practicing and set the example. We cannot expect to receive affirmation and truth if we are not willing to give that to others.

* * *

Don't ever assume people know how you feel. When my husband and I were first married, I thought if he truly loved me he would know what I needed to be happy. Looking back, I realize I didn't even know what I needed to be happy. I spent a lot of unnecessary time upset before I realized he couldn't read my mind. This is true for anyone in your life, whether it is a significant other, friend, family member, neighbor or co-worker. Don't expect anyone to be able to read your mind. Ask for what you need. Out loud. In your grown-up voice.

Step Four:

Surround Yourself with Support

(Who's Your Scarecrow?)

* * *

You don't have to do this alone. You can, but you don't have to. Know that there are people who want to help you. Look for them and you will find them (although they may not always be who or what you expected them to be).

* * *

When Dorothy started going down the yellow brick road, the Scarecrow was the first to try and help. He admitted he had his own problems and didn't know exactly what to do, but he was there and willing to take the steps down that path with her. The people who come into our lives and are willing to be there during tough times are more valuable than they realize. It's comforting just to know we aren't alone.

* * *

The Tin Men in our lives are the ones who have the tools to clear the way. They can help us to chip away at the obstacles in our path. They can also use their tools to protect us when we need it.

* * *

The Lions that show up to help us may not think of themselves as being brave, but there's something about them that commands the attention of others around them. They have an air of authority. They know how to roar when they need to…and there will be times when you need someone willing to roar for you!

* * *

We need our "Totos" too. Totos are those in our lives who love us unconditionally and accept us with unfailing devotion, no matter what we've done or failed to do. Our Toto may be a friend, a spouse, a child, or even a pet. When the tough times come, our Toto may be the only one who keeps us going by seeing our value even when we can't.

* * *

Seek out the people who can support you and help you through the tough times. If you don't have friends or family who are available to fill those roles for the situation you are going through, there are many agencies, organizations, support groups and hotlines specifically designed for this purpose. Call them. Sometimes this is exactly the place where your Glinda the Good Witch will appear!

Step Five:

Avoid Negative Influences

(Beware of Flying Monkeys!)

* * *

Dorothy was making pretty good progress in her journey to Oz when, out of the blue, flying monkeys swooped down, grabbed her and took her to a dark and scary place. There may be a few flying monkeys in your life right now too. Negative people can rob you of your strength and hope. You need both when you are trying to get to a better place. It's important to surround yourself with the people who can help you stay positive and productive.

* * *

It's a hard fact of life that not everyone has your best interests in mind. Flying Monkeys may think they are doing what they are supposed to do, but can definitely make the situation worse. In times when we need them the most, they tend to give the things we need the least. While they may be well intentioned, their interference can block our progress.

* * *

Monkeys come in all shapes, sizes, and disguises. Some treat you differently just because you are facing tough times. Some withdraw and avoid you because your situation makes them uncomfortable. Some are overly eager to point out painful information. Some may tell you that if you were just tougher or braver or smarter, you wouldn't be where you are now.

* * *

Monkeys may encourage you to give up - or settle for less than you deserve - or accept things the way they are no matter what toll it takes on your life. They may want you to stay where you are because it serves some purpose for them. A Flying Monkey is anyone who makes you question your own value, power or options in life.

* * *

Just as they did with Dorothy, Flying Monkeys have a way of taking you to the places you fear and just leaving you there. Flying Monkeys may not mean to harm you. As hurtful as it may seem when you are suffering, you need to understand there are times when others simply do not recognize how or why you need their help.

* * *

Acknowledging the monkeys in our lives helps us to recognize them when they show up. If we can recognize them, we can learn to do what we need to do in spite of their negative influences. While some monkeys show up completely out of the blue, others show up over and over again. When our "resident monkeys" show up we say, "I can't believe they did that - didn't do that - said that…" (You fill in the blank). Why not? Haven't they done it before? Isn't it likely they will do it again? Stop being surprised by consistent behaviors. It's like an adult version of peek-a-boo with pain.

* * *

Stop letting the monkeys ambush you. Be prepared for monkeys by having strategies for handling them. If you don't feel like you have the strength or energy to deal with the monkeys in your life, then maybe you should think about not hanging out at the zoo (or other places where monkeys tend to be).

* * *

 Even people we love, (and who love us) can be the monkeys in our lives at one time or another.

* * *

It may be a good idea to get a mirror and take a good long look at yourself. Be honest. If you are the one who's been hijacking your own hopes and dreams, then you have to face up to it before you can fix it.

* * *

We become our own monkeys with self-defeating behaviors like abuse, negative attitudes, anger, self-pity and blame. You can't deal with anyone else's monkey until you deal with your own.

* * *

Get in touch with your inner monkey; acknowledge it, confront it, grab it by the tail and get it back in line. You cannot change anything unless - and until - you are willing to change.

Some Monkey Handling Tips…...

Although these strategies may not change the monkeys you encounter, they may help prevent them from blocking your progress. Here are some basic principles of monkey behavior:

1. Monkeys do things for their own reasons, not yours. Most negative behaviors are responses to fear or pain in their lives. Don't take their behavior personally. It's not so much about you as it is about them.
2. You cannot change someone else's behavior. You **can** change the way you respond to it.
3. Negative behaviors decrease – and sometimes disappear - when you no longer give the monkeys the response they are seeking.
4. Dealing with monkeys takes practice and patience. Don't get discouraged. It's worth all the efforts when behaviors change.

With those things in mind, here are some things you **can** do:

Don't be afraid to ask for what you need. Sometimes others just don't know what to do to help.

When the "monkey behaviors" begin to appear, create a distraction or change the subject. Try using humor or finding points you can agree on to disarm them.

Praise and reinforce the behaviors that are more appropriate and supportive. Negative behaviors are generally a cry for attention. Giving attention for positive behaviors reduces negative behaviors.

Try and identify any areas of insecurity that may be prompting the monkey behavior and openly discuss it with them. (Example: "Are you afraid that what's going on with me will change your life in some way?")

Stand up to them, but don't fight. Your goal is to express your needs and feelings. This is not a battle of right and wrong.

Don't assume they do negative things just to hurt you. Bring negative behaviors to their attention and discuss them. Openly addressing the issue can guide you to greater understanding.

Step Six:

Keep Moving Forward

(The Emerald City is in Sight!)

* * *

Dorothy must have felt pretty helpless when she landed in Oz. Everything was different. She was forced to deal with an unfamiliar situation in an unfamiliar place. She had no idea what to do. You may feel the same way. Helplessness can be a terrible feeling. There may be things you can't do anything about right now. That's okay. Focus on what you CAN do and do it. The rest will come.

* * *

Nothing is hopeless. Refuse to believe anyone or anything that makes you feel differently. Situations can happen - or build up - in our lives that completely block our ability to see beyond them, but NOTHING is hopeless.

* * *

No matter how slim or faraway it seems, hold on to hope with everything you've got. It can take you places greater than you ever imagined!

* * *

The thing is, (and pay close attention here because this is the part most people don't get) you can't just sit there and wait for opportunities to fall at your feet. You have to reach out and grab them when they come by. **You've got to do your part**.

* * *

It doesn't matter what someone else may have done, or not done, in the past. It's not up to them to fix your life. It's up to you.

* * *

With this in mind, understand you can **only** do **your** part. You cannot be responsible for what other people need to do. Sound simple? It's not. But it gets easier with practice. Do what you can and keep moving forward.

ALL I CAN DO IS ALL I CAN DO...AND ALL I CAN DO IS ENOUGH

* * *

Be realistic and recognize your limits. We all have limits. There's no need to give up just because you can't do it all, be it all, have it all. There was a time in my life when I literally had to print a sign to put on the wall over my desk that said, "All I can do is all I can do…and all I can do is enough." I used it to remind myself that some things are simply beyond the scope of what I can do. I can't control what others do or do not do. I can't put more than 24 hours in a day. I can't control the weather or the economy or life or death or hormones. I am responsible for doing everything I possibly can to accomplish my goals, but when I have honestly done that, it's enough.

* * *

Don't let fear stop you. Fear is the opposite of faith. It is believing the worst will happen instead of working for the best.

* * *

Like Dorothy and her friends, sometimes the path to where you want to be can take you through some frightening places. You may encounter obstacles. It may not be lions or tigers or bears, but there's some pretty scary stuff out there. Hang in there. Sometimes survival is just a matter of endurance. Take the steps you need to take. When we take risks, we open ourselves up to greater possibilities.

* * *

When Dorothy finally confronted the Wicked Witch head on, she was able to stop her and take her power away. Face **your** fears by taking a closer look at them. Ask for help in doing this if you need it. Fear can be one of the biggest roadblocks in our path. When you confront your fears, you may find they aren't as powerful or frightening as you once believed. Keep in mind this common acronym for fear: **F**alse **E**vidence **A**ppearing **R**eal. Fears are frequently based on misinformation, misconceptions and irrational thoughts.

* * *

The majority of things we spend time worrying about never happen. Put your energy into the things you can do something about and you'll have less time (and fewer reasons) to worry.

Step Seven:

Acknowledge Your Inner Power

(Click Those Ruby Slippers!)

* * *

Dorothy's journey to Oz and back helped her realize some valuable information about her life. Your journey can do the same for you. Take time to be still and listen to the life lessons and wisdom you already possess. Your life is the result of choices you have made or failed to make. You have the power to change it with each new choice you make.

* * *

Once you begin to identify and eliminate the beliefs that have limited you in the past, you will realize you have more options and opportunities for the future than you ever imagined. The answers to all our problems, hopes and dreams, lie within us. When you begin to understand this and trust it, you truly begin to allow yourself to become all you want to be.

* * *

As Dorothy and each of her companions came to realize, facing challenges helps us to recognize we have more love (heart), wisdom (brains) and courage than we ever imagined.

Love goes beyond the limits of understanding. You don't have to have proof it's there. You just have to stop questioning and start trusting.

Courage is nothing more than doing what you need to do even when you are afraid.

Wisdom is understanding the difference between what's important and what's not.

The love, courage and wisdom you gain from going through difficult times gives you the ability to make the differences in your life you once felt were impossible.

* * *

Recognize what is true in your life. The Wizard didn't give Dorothy and her friends the things they sought. He simply pointed out qualities they already possessed. Dorothy had the power to go home; she just didn't know it. When Dorothy got back to Kansas, nothing had changed, not even the people who surrounded her. She just had the opportunity to see them in a different light.

* * *

Claim the result you want to see. I once sat at a table surrounded by medical professionals and listened to them one by one saying there was no hope for the situation we faced. One of them literally said, "Expect the worst." It turned out, they were wrong, and whether you want to call it a miracle or not, the situation completely turned around. You have to decide how to process the information you are given. If you can do that without giving up, you may also have the opportunity to see that even in seemingly hopeless situations, things can turn around. Hope is a powerful thing. It is an ingredient essential to overcoming unintended and unwanted life circumstances. Hope can lead ordinary people to greatness. The lack of it can destroy lives. I believe it is the defining difference in our lives.

* * *

Your life is a statement of who you are. If you feel resistance when reading these words, you need to go back, highlight them, and start putting some serious thought into why it makes you uncomfortable. If there are things in your life right now that do not truly reflect the person you want to be, then it may be time to think about any changes you need to make to become that person you have in mind.

* * *

As things get easier, (and they will), take time to appreciate them. No matter how small each step forward is, know it is one step closer to your goal. Acknowledge it. Embrace it. Celebrate it. There is great power in gratitude.

* * *

Gratitude is recognition that even in a world where so many things seem to go wrong, there are still many things going right. It opens our hearts to things greater than ourselves.

* * *

Gratitude unexpressed is like a gift unopened. Its true value cannot be realized unless shared.

* * *

The very things that appear to limit us may be exactly what we need to put us on the path to becoming the individuals we are truly meant to be.

* * *

Crisis and challenge give you the option of reevaluating what is important to you. In helping to change your perspective, they can help you change the things you may have settled for, or taken for granted in the past. Challenges inevitably change you, but whether that change is for better or for worse is up to you.

* * *

Ruby slippers, no matter how pretty and shiny, are not always the best choice to get you to the places you want to go. Yeah, they may look good, and you may look good and feel good in them, but at the end of the day if the fit isn't right you may end up in a lot of pain (especially if you plan on covering a lot of territory, skipping and dancing along uneven surfaces). Whether you are making a decision about footwear or life direction, you have to consider the long-term consequences and not just the short-term benefits.

* * *

Understand that the things that make you happy don't have to meet everyone else's expectations. What makes you happy doesn't have to make sense to everyone else. Happiness isn't measured by monumental achievements…it's measured in moments. It's not nearly as complicated as we tend to make it.

* * *

Know that you can get through this. There is something to give and something to gain in every situation that comes your way. Find the gift in this. Give meaning to the struggles you go through by using the strength and knowledge you gain to help yourself and others. Challenges can be the pivotal points in our lives. Each choice we consider, any challenge we undertake, every decision we make, defines who we are.

* * *

What you allow yourself to learn from overcoming obstacles can transform your life from ordinary to extraordinary. Taking the steps to find your way back from places we never intended to be may not be easy, but it's worth it. One step at a time, one day at a time, breathe in, breathe out, put on clean underwear, keep moving forward and know you can do this! GOOD LUCK!

Resources For Finding Your Way

Recognizing Your Resources…

Most of us hate to ask for help - or we don't know how - or we never even see it as an option. I'm telling you that you not only have a right to ask for the help you need, you SHOULD ask for help. No one should face every situation alone.

Family members may be the first ones who come to mind to ask for help (or the last, depending on your particular situation), but it's important to remember that our family isn't just made up of people related to us. You may have a church family, work family, school family or family of friends. "Family" is anyone who cares about you. If they care about you, they want to help. It's up to you to help them know what to do. If friends and family aren't available here are some other resources to try:

The Library: Your local library has an abundance of information.

The Internet: Nearly unlimited information awaits you on the internet.

The Phone Book: Check the yellow-page listings to find organizations that offer support.

Local Resource Centers: Most agencies offer resource lists for support groups and other services.

Churches: Many churches, synagogues, or other spiritual centers have someone who can not only lend a sympathetic ear, but can also help you to find the information and resources you need.

When you need specific information…

The following organizations can provide information, resources and referrals:

National Institute of Mental Health: 1-866-615-6464 or www.nimh.nih.gov

Mental Health America: 1-800-969-6642 or www.nmha.org

Anxiety Disorders Association of America: 240-485-1001 or www.adaa.org

Suicide Prevention Hotline: 1-800-273-8255 or www.suicidepreventionlifeline.org

Substance Abuse and Mental Health Resources: www.samhsa.gov

Grief Net: (an internet community dealing with grief, death and loss) www.griefnet.org

About the Author

Sharon Yates has spent over thirty years working as a Mental Health Professional. After earning a Social Work degree from East Carolina University, she began a career of helping people that includes roles as counselor, consultant, trainer, supervisor and manager. In her current role as Public Relations Director for the Cumberland County Mental Health Center, Sharon coordinates events, disseminates information, promotes mental health services and produces a public-access cable television show, "Focus on Mental Health." Her first book, *The Busy Mom*, was released by Child and Family Press, a division of The Child Welfare League of America, (Washington, D.C.) in 2002. She lives in Fayetteville, North Carolina, with her husband Steve and son James and is surrounded by family and friends who help her – every day – to appreciate the important things in life.

About the Illustrator

Rose-Ann San Martino has been involved in the worlds of art, theatre and mental health for many years. She has lived in Washington, D.C. and Cambridge, MA where she worked building and painting theater sets, and creating props for various productions, including those at the Boston Children's Museum and the USS Constitution Museum. She has taught theater and art to at-risk youth and designed the 1992 Boston Marathon T-shirt. Since moving to Fayetteville her uniquely styled paintings have been exhibited in solo and group shows in various art venues throughout the city. She lives with her wonderful husband, Stan, two dogs, two cats and a bunch of fish.